D1393580

Christmas Recipes

Christmas Recipes

written out in manuscript form
and illustrated by
George L Thomson
scribe

Canongate
Edinburgh
1980

First published in 1980
by
Canongate Publishing Ltd.
17 Jeffrey Street
Edinburgh

© Canongate Publishing 1980
ISBN 0 86241 005 3

Printed and bound in Great Britain
by
T. & A. Constable Ltd.
Hopetoun Street, Edinburgh

Contents

North Pole ⁂ Arctic

Christmas Eve

(Phew - bloomin' soot! I'm so damn busy - sleigh needs a new
runner, poor reindeer never have enough lichen, too many presents
and to top it all the gnomes are on a go-slow.

So I haven't got much time to tell you about my Christmas Recipes;
unlike all you lucky folk, I haven't even got time to cook any of
these delicious meals. I do all my cooking in the summer, back
home at the North Pole, where my old friend George wrote down
these recipes for me.

(But I HAVE got time to tell you that Christmas will never be the same
again once you have a copy of my ancient and delicious Christmas
fare! My beard quivers at the thought of all those magnificent
aromas wafting round the world, while I have to tackle all your
filthy chimneys.

What would Christmas be without ME? I am really very important,
so don't forget to write me a letter, and please leave some food for me
and my reindeer, and DO clean out your chimney, and remember
to hang up your sock [be sure it's WASHED!] and .... oh, almost forgot!
HAVE A WONDERFUL CHRISTMAS!
Love

Father Christmas

Roast Turkey

✦

Preheat oven to 325°, Gas No 3, and allow 25 minutes per lb and 20 minutes over.

Stuff the turkey at both ends with your preferred stuffing. Put in a large meat tin and smooth all over with melted butter. Sprinkle the top and sides with pepper. Place a double layer of foil over the breast as the legs take longer to cook. Loosely cover over all with foil. Place in the oven and cook for the prescribed time, basting every half hour, and removing the foil one hour before cooking time is completed. Place a buttered paper over the breast.

To test when the bird is done, pierce a leg with a fine skewer. If no pink liquid runs out, it is cooked. Cooking for too long makes the bird dry. Remove from the oven and put on to a hot dish. Sprinkle lightly with salt, and replace the foil.

Roast Goose

This does not go as far as turkey but it is richer

Preheat oven to 350°, Gas № 4, and allow 25 minutes per pound and 20 minutes over. You will need a 10 lb bird for six to eight people.

Stuff the bird with your preferred stuffing. Prick the fat area [near the legs and wings] with a needle, and smooth all over with a good cooking oil. Shake a little pepper over top. Place in a large meat tin, cover loosely with foil and place in oven. Baste every half hour. After 1½ hours remove the foil and return to oven.

When cooked, season well with salt and a little more pepper. Sprinkle with lemon juice. Remove to a hot dish and cover.

Pour off fat from meat tin, but leave the meaty substance for gravy. Put this over heat and add 1 dessertspoon of flour, stir and let it brown. Season and add 1 pint stock or vegetable water gradually. Continue stirring until it thickens slightly.

Baked Ham

An essential for the Christmas Season

1 large ham 6–18 lbs · 1 dsstsp peppercorns · 2 crushed bay leaves · 6 cloves · melted honey · 4 oz soft brown sugar · cider vinegar · 1 tsp dry mustard · ground black pepper · grated nutmeg · chopped pineapple or redcurrant jelly and chopped raisins

❖

Soak ham overnight; if very salty, soak 12 hours during the day, changing water twice. Put in a large pan or fish kettle and cover with cold water, peppercorns, bay leaves and cloves. Cover & bring to boil. Skim, cover and simmer. For a 6 lb ham, allow 25 minutes per lb; for a larger one only 15 minutes per lb. Test before removing from pan. When ready place on dish or board and remove outer skin – gently so as not to pull off the fat. Lightly score the fat in 1" diamond pattern. Brush whole ham with melted honey. Mix soft brown sugar with enough cider vinegar to moisten, add dry mustard, a little black pepper and grated nutmeg. Spread over ham. Stick whole cloves in each diamond shape. Bake in moderate oven, Gas № 4 until golden. Serve with fresh chopped pineapple, or hot redcurrant jelly to which chopped raisins and a little wine have been added

This ham is particularly delicious cold

3

Gravy

Giblet stock · ½ glass red wine · 1 level tblsp plain flour · 1 large tsp cranberry sauce · salt & pepper to taste

✦

Make some stock out of your turkey giblets on christmas Eve! When the turkey is cooked, remove from its roasting pan. Drain excess fat from the pan, but be careful to keep all the juices, brown skin etc..

Over a very gentle heat add the plain flour, mixing it into the juices until a creamy consistency is reached. Slowly pour in some stock, stirring all the time. Add the wine, still stirring, and then the rest of the stock or as much as required. Simmer for two minutes while cranberry sauce and seasoning is added.

Pour through a coarse sieve before serving in a heated gravy boat or jug.

Chicken Liver Pate

1 lb chicken livers · 3/4 lb butter · 2 medium sized onions · 1 bay leaf · freshly ground black pepper · 2 large cloves of garlic

Boil the livers for five minutes in salted water. Drain and allow to cool a little. Remove the skins and trim. Sieve them into a bowl. Chop the onions, bay leaf and garlic very finely, and fry them very gently in a half pound of butter until they are just soft. Pour all this over the sieved chicken livers, and mix together using plenty of black pepper. Pack tightly into one or two suitable pots and pour the remaining quarter pound of melted butter over the top to seal.

Serve cold with toast and butter

Partridge Pie

Partridges should be hung for a week approximately, before being plucked and cooked.

2 partridges · ¼ lb butter · ½ lb lean pork · 2 rashers bacon ·
2 hardboiled eggs · 3 oz mushrooms · 1 onion · ¼ pint of stock ·
¼ pint red wine · 4 – 6 oz puff pastry · seasoning · 1 beaten
egg

❖

Cut partridges in quarters and fry in butter until browned.
Place in a pie-dish and add the pork, cut into thin strips. Chop
the bacon coarsely and lay over the meat, then add the coarsely
chopped eggs. Chop up the onions and mushrooms and sprinkle
on top, season, and add the stock and wine. Roll out the pastry,
making it a little wider than the top of the pie-dish. Cut the
edge off the pastry, dampen the edge of the dish and press the
thin edge of pastry round it. Place the rest of the pastry over the
top, trim round the edges and press together. Make a hole in
the centre, and decorate with scraps of pastry made into leaf
shapes. Brush with beaten egg, and cook till brown at Gas № 6,
450°F. Reduce the heat, cover the pie with greaseproof paper,
and continue to cook until it has been in the oven for two hours.

This seasonal pie can be eaten hot or cold.

6

Roast Chicken

If there are only one or two of you, a roast chicken makes a good traditional lunch for Christmas Day

1 plump chicken · 3 rashers streaky bacon · a few chipolata sausages · 1 lemon · a little chicken giblet stock · 1 glass white wine · vegetable oil · 1 tsp tarragon · 1 dsstsp flour · ¼ lb butter

Pour a little oil into a roasting pan and put in the chicken. Cut the lemon in half and squeeze a little of the juice over the bird. Put the lemon halves inside the chicken. Mash the tarragon and butter together and add to the lemon halves. This is not a conventional stuffing, but it gives the chicken a wonderful fresh flavour. Use one of the other stuffings given in this book if you want more variety. Sprinkle a little more tarragon over the bird, lay the bacon rashers over the top and the sausages round the side. Cover loosely with tinfoil which you should remove before it is done. Cook in a fairly hot oven for about one hour.

To make a sauce: place the bird on a dish, pouring the liquids out of the chicken into the roasting pan. Stir in a little flour and slowly add the wine and stock until a creamy consistency is achieved.

Baked Halibut in Cream

Many people consider halibut to be the finest of white fish. This recipe makes a superb meal for the festive season and provides a welcome change. Halibut are not always easy to find, and it is essential to give your fishmonger several days warning.

1 whole halibut · 2 bay leaves · dill · sprigs of fresh rosemary · 2 egg yolks · ¼ lb butter · ¼ pint milk · ½ pint cream · ½ lb shrimps · salt · freshly ground black pepper

Clean the fish, and in its centre place the dill, bay leaves, half of the shrimps and 2 oz butter. Put it in a large baking tray and dot the remaining butter and a little more dill, salt & pepper over the top. Cover loosely with tinfoil and bake until the fish comes off the bone easily, at Gas Nº 4, 360°F. The time varies enormously depending on the size of the fish.

When cooked, place the fish on a large flat dish. Put the baking tray on a low heat and mix the cream and the egg yolks in with the milk. Do not allow to boil. Stir in the rest of the shrimps gently, adding a little more ground pepper and salt to taste. Pour this sauce over the fish and place some little sprigs of fresh rosemary over the top and round the sides, then serve immediately.

Turkey Fricassée

1 lb turkey leftovers · 1 large onion · ¼ lb butter · 1 tblsp finely chopped celery leaves · freshly ground black pepper · a touch of chilli powder · sage · salt · ½ pint single cream · turkey stock

Chop the onion and fry it gently in the butter until just soft. Add the rest of the ingredients except the stock and the cream. Turn it all carefully until it is thoroughly heated, then add the cream, and enough stock to make it all of a creamy consistency. Serve with mushrooms, peas and a salad.

Potted Cheese

2 oz Cheddar cheese · 2 oz cheshire cheese · 2 oz Stilton cheese ·
3 oz softened butter · chopped parsley · chopped chives or onion ·
3 tblsp port · 1 tblsp cream

Grate the cheese finely and mix well. Add the butter and cream and mix thoroughly. Finally add the chopped parsley and chives with the port and again mix thoroughly. Press into a pot and cover tightly, then store in a cool place.

Tomato Mousse

This is a very decorative dish suitable for a first course. Enough for 8 people

2lbs ripe but firm tomatoes · 1 dsstsp lemon juice · 1 tsp grated rind · 1 dsstsp orange juice · 1 tsp grated rind · 1 tsp chopped sweet basil · ¼ tsp sea salt · ground green pepper to taste · ½ tsp castor sugar · 3 envelopes or 9 tsp powdered gelatine · ½ pt approx. dry white wine · ¼ pt approx. water · 1 green pepper for decoration

❖

Cut tomatoes in quarters and place in saucepan with lemon and orange juice and rinds, salt, pepper, sugar and water, and bring to boil. Simmer until tender. Strain through medium sieve. Put gelatine in small bowl, add ¼ pint wine. Leave until absorbed, then place over hot, not boiling water until it liquefies. Add this to the warm tomato mixture, with the basil and ground green pepper. Measure and make up to 2 pints with the rest of the wine and more water if necessary. Pour into a wetted ring mould, 2 pints capacity, and leave till set in cold room or refrigerator. To turn out, dip mould in hot water for a few seconds. Ease round the rim with a knife. Turn on to a plate. If it fails to come out, place a hot cloth on top of ring to loosen it.

Decorate with green pepper cut into holly leaf shapes, and round the edge with fingers of toast.

11

Turkey Mould

8 oz left-over turkey · 4 oz cooked ham · 2 tomatoes · 2 sticks celery · 2 eggs · 2 oz butter · 3 oz flour · ¾ pint of stock · salt · pepper

✥

Mince the turkey, ham, tomatoes and celery. Beat the eggs. Melt the butter in a pan and add the flour. Cook gently, but do not allow to brown. Add stock and stir well. Cook until thick. Add the eggs, stirring all the time. When the mixture is quite smooth, add the minced ingredients and season to taste. Turn into a greased soufflé dish and cover with greaseproof paper. Bake in a moderate oven, Gas № 3, 320,° for 1½ hours. Leave to get cold, then turn out on to a plate.

Ham Mousse

1½ lbs cooked ham · 1 tsp made mustard · 2 tblsp powdered gelatine · ¼ breakfastcup cold water · ½ breakfastcup of hot water · 1 breakfastcup cream · 1 green pepper · parsley

Pound the ham and mix in the mustard. Soak the gelatine in the cold water, then dissolve in the hot water. Add to the ham. Blend in the stiffly beaten cream. Chop the green pepper and mix with the other ingredients. Put into a wetted mould and allow to set. Turn out, garnish with parsley and serve with horseradish cream.

Horseradish Cream

2 tsp grated horseradish · ¼ pint thick cream · salt

Thoroughly mix together all the above ingredients

Turkey Soup

Put the turkey carcase, together with any left-over stuffing, potatoes and other vegetables and gravy into a large pan. Cover with cold water, add salt and pepper and one dessert spoonful of vinegar. Bring to the boil, and simmer for three hours, or put into oven at Gas № 2, turning to № 1 after one hour. Strain into a bowl and leave until cold. Skim off the fat. Heat and serve with cubes of toasted bread which have been tossed in simmering butter.

For a slightly more exotically flavoured soup, add cloves of garlic, peppercorns and a bay leaf to the stock, and add a glass or two of a red wine fifteen minutes before removing from the heat.

Chestnut Soup

2 pints stock [chicken gives best results] · ½ lb chestnuts ·
1 medium onion · 1 oz butter · salt · pepper · 1 egg yolk · fresh
cream

Prick chestnuts and boil for half an hour. Cool and remove
skins. Slice the onion thinly and fry gently in butter until
soft, but do not brown. Add the chestnuts and stock, and
seasoning if necessary, then boil until the chestnuts are soft.
Rub through a sieve. Beat the egg yolk well and add the
cream. Stir gently into soup and continue stirring for five
minutes over very gentle heat. Serve with fried croutons.

Cranberry Sauce

This is a pure but delectable recipe traditionally used in North America to accompany the roast turkey

½ pint water · ½ lb sugar · ½ lb whole cranberries · port optional

✤

Melt the sugar in the water and boil for three or four minutes, then add the cranberries and simmer until the berries burst

Serve cold

Add port if you would like a richer, more exotic flavour

Italian Stuffing

½ lb chipolata sausages · ½ lb boiled & peeled chestnuts, crushed ·
6 stoned prunes chopped up coarsely · 2 oz butter · 4 pears, peeled &
quartered · turkey's liver, blanched and coarsely chopped · 1 glass
white wine

❖

Half cook the sausages, let them cool, skin them and cut into
little round slices.   Melt the butter in a saucepan and
add the sausage slices, prunes, pears, chestnuts and turkey
liver.   Pour off any excess butter and add in the white wine.
Stuff this into the smaller end of the turkey.

Sausage Meat Stuffing

for Turkey

½ lb pork sausage meat · 1 tblsp soft breadcrumbs · pinch mixed herbs · grated rind of ½ lemon & juice · salt · pepper

Thoroughly mix together all the above ingredients.

Forcemeat Stuffing

traditional stuffing for turkey breast

½ lb breadcrumbs · ½ lb butter · 1 tsp lemon juice · grated rind of 1 lemon · 2 eggs, lightly mixed · 4 tblsp parsley finely chopped · ¼ tsp thyme · ¼ tsp mixed herbs · salt · pepper

Mix together breadcrumbs, parsley, thyme, herbs, lemon rind, salt and pepper. Add melted butter, eggs and lemon juice, and mix well. Sufficient to stuff a 15 lb turkey.

18

Apricot Stuffing

for Goose

1 lb dried tart apricots [obtainable at natural food shops] · 4 oz bread crumbs · 1 onion · 1 apple · 2 eggs · 3 oz butter · salt · pepper · celery seed

Soak the apricots for eight hours. Chop and mix with the unpeeled chopped apple. Add breadcrumbs, beaten eggs, melted butter and seasoning.

Apple & Celery Stuffing

for Goose

1 cooking apple · small head of celery

Chop the apple and celery and proceed as for apricot stuffing.

Gooseberry stuffing : substitute cooked and sugared gooseberries for the apricots, and follow the same proceedure

19

Sage & Onion Stuffing

for Turkey

1 lb onions · 4 oz breadcrumbs · ½ oz butter · 2 or 3 sprigs sage
or 1 tsp powdered sage

Peel slice and chop the onions. Warm the butter in a pan,
add the onions and cook gently, being careful not to brown.
When tender, mix all together.

Parsley & Thyme Stuffing

Prepare as above, but leave out the sage and add a little
thyme.

Chestnut Stuffing

for Turkey

2 lbs dried chestnuts [most shops have these ready peeled]. ½ lb sausage meat · ½ pint stock or milk · 1 oz butter · pepper · salt

❖

Soak the chestnuts overnight. Place in a pan of water and bring to the boil. Simmer until tender. Break up coarsely with a fork and mash into the sausage meat, adding softened butter and seasoning. Mix well and place in the turkey.

❖

Chestnut Stuffing 2

Sufficient for a 6 lb bird; double quantities for a large turkey

8 oz chestnuts · 1 oz butter · 2 oz fresh white breadcrumbs · 1 tsp freshly chopped parsley · 1 egg · salt · pepper · ½ pint of stock

❖

Skin the chestnuts and boil in stock until they are tender and all the liquid has been absorbed. Rub through a sieve! Add the melted butter, salt and pepper, parsley and bread crumbs, and bind together with beaten egg.

❖

Savoury Sausage Meat Stuffing

2 lbs pork sausage meat · ¼ lb streaky bacon · 1 large onion · 1 tsp powdered sage or rosemary · ½ oz butter

Fry chopped bacon and finely chopped onion in butter until soft. Do not brown. Mix sausage meat and herbs and add bacon and onion. Mix well. Sufficient to stuff a 15 lb turkey.

Bread Sauce

1 cupful white bread · ½ pint milk · small onion stuck with a few cloves · pinch of nutmeg · blade of mace · knob of butter · salt · pepper

Put everything except the butter into a suitable pan and bring to the boil. Simmer until the onion is well cooked. If the sauce is too thick, add more milk. Before serving, add butter and remove the onion, and then stir lightly.

Bread Sauce 2

1 pt milk · 1 onion stuck with cloves · 1 piece of mace · pepper · salt · knob of butter · 2 cups roughly cut white country bread

Simmer the onion in milk with the mace and seasoning for fifteen minutes.   Add the pieces of bread.   Just before serving, stir in the butter.

Beetroot Shape

(Excellent with cold turkey

2 lbs beetroot · 2 eating apples · 1 tblsp softened butter · 1 dsstsp cider vinegar

Cut beetroot and apples into small pieces and put through a mincer.   Stir butter and cider vinegar into the beetroot. Press into a lightly buttered pudding basin and cover top with greaseproof paper.   Steam until hot.   Turn out and serve either hot or cold.

24

Brussels Sprouts with Chestnuts

THE traditional Christmas vegetable

1 lb Brussels sprouts · ½ lb chestnuts · 2 oz butter · 1 or 2 tblsp of cream [optional] · salt · pepper

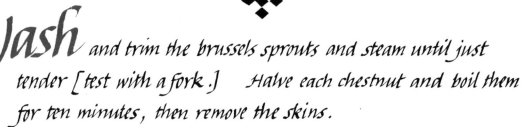

Wash and trim the brussels sprouts and steam until just tender [test with a fork.] Halve each chestnut and boil them for ten minutes, then remove the skins.

Heat the butter in a thick pan and season with salt and pepper. Add the chestnuts, cover the pan and cook until tender. Add the brussels sprouts and continue cooking for five minutes.

Put in cream now if liked, and heat but do not allow to boil.

Flaming Chestnuts

One pound of chestnuts, peeled and soaked in cold water until fairly tender. Bring to the boil and simmer for five minutes, then pierce with a darning needle to see if they are completely tender. Drain and place in a warm salad bowl. Sprinkle with icing sugar. Pour over a wineglass of warmed rum, and light before serving.

Vegetable Leftovers

Grease a large frying pan and put in any chopped left over vegetables such as sprouts, cabbage and carrots. Add 2 oz softened butter and a finely chopped onion. Fry gently to brown underneath and put under grill till golden brown. According to amount of vegetables used extra butter may have to be dotted on top before grilling. Loosen sides and underneath with a palette knife and turn quickly on to a hot dish.

Red Cabbage

1 red cabbage · ½ cup water · 3 oz butter · 1 large onion · 1 cooking apple · 1 dsstsp flour [heaped] · seasoning · 2 tblsp wine vinegar · sour cream if liked

✦

Shred finely a whole red cabbage but cut out the hard white core. Melt 2 oz butter in a large pan and add diced onion. Cook gently and add chopped cabbage, chopped apple and water. This should be cooked for 15 minutes. Mix the flour and 1 oz butter together over a gentle heat and add to cabbage mixture whilst simmering, and stir until all thickens. Season and add the wine vinegar. Can be served either hot or cold. Sour cream may be stirred in before serving if liked. This keeps well for seven days.

Pineapple Salad

2 or 3 shredded crisp lettuce hearts · cubed fresh pineapple · mayonnaise

First make mayonnaise as for walnut and apple salad. Put shredded lettuce and cubed pineapple into a salad bowl and sprinkle with salt to taste. Add mayonnaise gradually.

Cabbage Salad

Choose a white crisp cabbage and shred very finely. Make a French dressing with a good quality oil and lemon juice. Season and mix together. This is delicious with a small carton of plain yogurt, salt & pepper, and a squeezed clove of garlic.

Walnut & Apple Salad

2lbs eating apples, unpeeled, chopped · 1 cup walnuts coarsely chopped · ½ cup finely chopped celery · ½ cup of mayonnaise

✛

First make mayonnaise by whisking two raw egg yolks with a little salt and pepper. The eggs must be at room temperature, otherwise the mixture will curdle. Now add drop by drop half a pint of good quality oil and stir continuously until thick. Add one to two teaspoonful of wine vinegar or lemon juice. Test for seasoning.

Put the chopped walnuts, celery and apples into a salad bowl and add mayonnaise gradually.

Christmas Pudding

This recipe is at least 300 years old, and makes a light textured, very dark pudding which will fade all others into insignificance

½ lb currants · ½ lb sultanas · ½ lb muscatel raisins, stoned · ½ lb fresh breadcrumbs · ½ lb demerara sugar · ½ lb grated suet · 1 large tsp mixed spice · 2 oz mixed peel · pinch salt · 6 eggs · 2 tblsp brandy, old beer or sherry

The above quantities will make a small pudding – 2¼ to 2½ pint basin size. It should be made at least 6 weeks before it is to be eaten, and is even more delicious if made a year or more in advance. It is therefore a good idea to make two years' supply at one time.

However big the quantities used, NEVER economise on the eggs – they make the pudding very dark and ensure its keeping qualities.

Choose a small basin which can be filled right to the brim with the mixture. Prepare a double sheet of greaseproof paper, large enough to overlap the basin. Grease well with beef dripping. Prepare a piece of clean white cotton or linen large enough to hold the basin. Flour well, and shake off surplus flour.

If necessary, clean the fruit with flour only over a sieve, shaking off surplus flour. Mix all dry ingredients together. Beat eggs & alcohol well and add to mixture. Stir thoroughly, cover with a

30

dry cloth, and leave overnight. Next morning, stir again, fill basin to the brim, even slightly over, smooth with a palette knife, cover with paper and cloth and tie down firmly. The diagonal ends of the cloth should be tied together to allow the basin to be lifted out of the boiling water easily after cooking.

Half fill a saucepan large enough to hold the basin on a rack, with water. Bring to boil and insert basin, then completely COVER basin and cloth with more boiling water. Cover with lid and boil for 10-12 hours, keeping the water bubbling gently. If the saucepan is too small for the water to cover the pudding, it can be STEAMED with the water only half way up. But it is better to cover it if possible. Top up when necessary with BOILING water.

Remove basin while water is still boiling, turn upside down on draining board, and leave until quite cold. Then remove cloth & paper and let the surface of the pudding dry slightly for an hour or so, lightly covered. Re-cover with paper & unfloured cloth. Store in a dry airy place, but not in a tin. It will keep for at least two years or more.

To re-heat, cover again with paper and floured cloth. Heat water as before and STEAM for 2-3 hours with water half way up. Turn out on to a hot dish. When it goes to the table, pour warmed brandy over it and immediately set alight with a match.

❖❖❖

❖ serve with brandy butter and/or whipped cream

❖❖

Snowballs

what shall we do with left-over Christmas Pudding? Here is one solution, and children often prefer it to the more conventional Christmas lunch pudding.

Left-over Christmas Pudding · 1 small handful icing sugar sieved

❖

Heat the Christmas Pudding mixture thoroughly. shape it into several balls about 1½" in diameter, keeping them hot as you do this. throw them one by one into the sieved icing sugar, making sure they are covered with a thick soft layer of whiteness.

Serve immediately

Snowy Mountain Dessert

¾ lb chestnuts · 1 carton double cream · 4 oz icing sugar · 2 oz castor sugar

Prick the chestnuts and boil for half an hour. Let them cool a little before skinning. Pass the peeled chestnuts through a sieve, then mix with the icing sugar. Pile the mixture into a steep mountain shape on a suitable plate. Whip the cream and add the castor sugar. Spread all over the mountain. Decorate the edges of the dish with little Christmas trees.

Frosted Grapes

Paint the grapes with lightly whipped egg white and immediately dip in sugar. Leave to dry.

Mincemeat

1lb finely chopped suet · 1lb currants · 1lb raisins · 1lb chopped apples · 1 lb castor sugar · ½ lb sultanas · ¼ lb shredded candied peel · 2 lemons · 1 tblsp brandy · 1 saltspoonful each of nutmeg, mace & cinnamon

Grate the lemon rind and squeeze the juice. Mix all the ingredients together thoroughly. Press into jars and cover. This mixture will keep for at least a month. These ingredients are sufficient to make 4–5 pounds of mincemeat.

Mince Pies

Rich Short Crust Paste for 12–18 pies

8 oz flour · 5 oz butter · 1 oz shortening or lard · 1 egg yolk · 2–3 tablespoons cold water · p. salt

Make pastry and chill. Roll out evenly and use two sizes of pastry cutters, a large one for the base and a smaller one to cover.

Toffee Sponge Pudding

4 oz self raising flour · 2 oz butter · 2 oz sugar · 1 egg · 2 tblsp milk · 2 tblsp syrup

Grease a pie dish and sprinkle with castor sugar, then pour in the warmed syrup. Cream the butter and sugar, add the well beaten egg and two tablespoons of flour. Stir well, adding milk and flour alternately and slowly. Beat until quite smooth. Bake for half an hour in a fairly hot oven, Gas mark № 5.

Mincemeat & Apple Turnover

6 oz mincemeat · 2 large cooking apples · 12 oz puff pastry · 2 tblsp soft brown sugar · 1 dsstsp brandy · a little milk · 1 egg yolk · castor sugar

Roll the pastry into an oblong, and spread the mincemeat, along with the cored, peeled and thinly sliced apples, down one side, only leaving sufficient pastry at the edges to close. Pour over the brandy and sugar. Fold over to form envelope and seal edges. Paint with egg yolk and scatter with castor sugar. Bake in a very hot oven for thirty minutes, and serve in slices with double cream, or with brandy butter!

Raspberry Trifle

Trifle sponges · 1 pt raspberry jelly, home-made if possible · 1 pt thick custard · 1 pt raspberry blancmange · 1 lb raspberries · ½ pt double cream · 1½ tablespoons sherry · angelica for decoration

❖

Place a layer of sponges in the bottom of a large glass bowl. Sprinkle with sherry and cover with a layer of raspberries. Make up jelly and when cooled pour over fruit. Leave to set. Meanwhile make one pint of raspberry blancmange and leave until almost cold. Spread the custard over the jelly, then the blancmange over the custard. Top with a thick layer of whipped cream, and decorate with raspberries and strips of angelica.

Orange & Lemon Icebergs

3 oranges · 3 lemons · 12 white marshmallows cut in quarters · 3 oz approx. gelatine · 4 oz approx. sugar · water

Cut the oranges in half. Squeeze out all the juice, being careful not to split the skins. Add enough water to the orange juice to make up half a pint. Heat the liquid but do not boil, and add sugar to taste. Add approximately 1½ oz gelatine, but be careful to follow the quantities on the packet as each brand varies. Sprinkle onto liquid and stir until dissolved. When the jelly has cooled but not set, pour into the orange halves, and put four pieces of marshmallow into each half.

Repeat this process for the lemons, making a little less than half a pint this time and adding more sugar. Cut a slice off the bottom of each lemon to make them stand firmly.

Liqueur Plum Preserve

12 Victoria plums · ½ lb warmed golden syrup · 12 cloves · ½ tea cup brandy · chopped almonds · quantity of meringue fingers

❖

Remove the stones from the plums, cut up and place in a bowl. Put the cloves in the syrup and heat gently. After five minutes remove the cloves and pour over fruit. When cold, stir in the half tea cup of brandy. The flavour is greatly improved if stored in a jar and kept for a few weeks. Serve in small glasses together with meringue fingers and sprinkle with chopped almonds.

Cherry Cake

½ lb flour · 1 tsp baking powder · ¼ lb butter · ¼ lb castor sugar · 2 eggs · 4 oz glace cherries, cut in halves · grated rind of ½ lemon · pinch of salt

Mix the flour, baking powder and salt together and sift. Add the grated lemon rind. Soften the butter until creamy and add the sugar. Beat for five minutes. Add the whipped up eggs gradually. When the mixture is smooth and creamy, start adding the flour and cherries, beating all the time. If the mixture is too thick, add a little milk. It should be soft enough to drop easily from a spoon. Line a baking tin, diameter 7" and 3" deep, with buttered greaseproof paper, pour in the mixture and bake for approximately one hour at 375°F. Gas № 4.

Brandy Butter

This can also be made with whisky or rum

6 oz butter · 8 oz icing sugar [sieved] · 2 tblsp brandy

Cream the butter thoroughly, then add the icing sugar fairly slowly, making it all an even consistency.

Finally beat in the brandy, very thoroughly.

Glacé Icing

1lb icing sugar · strained juice of half lemon · 3 fluid oz water, approx.

Sift the icing sugar into a bowl. Warm the liquids and pour on to the icing sugar. Beat well. If too runny, add more icing sugar. Pour over the almond paste already applied to your cake and let it run down the sides. Smooth off. A second coating can be added if a flat snowdrift effect is wanted.

42

Chocolate Log Cake

4 oz castor sugar · 1 dsstsp cocoa · pinch salt · 2 oz plain flour · 3 drops vanilla essence · chocolate butter cream for filling and covering

Warm sugar. (Prepare swiss roll tin 8" x 12". Oil tin and place greaseproof paper on top. Oil paper, being sure to cover sides & corners. Set oven at gas Mark 7 [425°].

Sift flour with salt & cocoa. Break eggs into a bowl, add warmed sugar and whip until thick and foamy. Add vanilla essence. Stir flour gently into foam, then spread all over tin into corners & place in oven.

Bake for 8-9 minutes, remove from oven and turn on to a sugared tea towel. Trim edges and roll up with the towel inside cake. When cool, unroll & fill with butter cream made with 6 oz softened butter, 12 oz icing sugar, 1 table—dessertspoonful cocoa according to taste, and vanilla essence. Some of this will go on top.

Fork along to resemble a tree trunk. The trimmed edges may be used to simulate "sawn off wood edges" and then recovered with the chocolate icing. A pleasing decoration could be meringue mushrooms, with ivy leaves cut out of boiled marzipan and green colouring added.

Sprinkle top of the cake with icing sugar to give the effect of snowflakes.

43

Iced Plum Pudding

A cool alternative to the traditional Christmas Pudding

2 eggs · 1 pt milk · 1 tblsp cornflour · ¼ lb sugar · vanilla essence ·
½ pt double cream · 1 tblsp each of chopped glacé cherries · angelica
glacé ginger · crystallized pineapple · currants · sultanas

❖

The fruit is covered with either sweet wine sherry or brandy
and should be left to soak for 8 hours.   Mix the
cornflour with a little of the milk to a paste.   Beat the
eggs well. Put the remainder of the milk with the sugar
into a saucepan and bring to the boil. Stir quickly into
the cornflour, add the beaten eggs and vanilla essence and
stir over a low flame for 10 minutes. Put into a basin and
let it get quite cold.

Lightly whip the cream & add. Pour into an ice container and
freeze softly. When lightly frozen turn out into a basin and whip
well to make the ice smooth. Add soaked fruit. Stir, return to ice
container & freeze hard. Scoop out into balls.

Alternatively, instead of pouring into the ice container, place
in a pudding basin, freeze and then turn out whole.

Sprinkle grated chocolate on top

44

Batter Cake

A mouth-watering cake, very rich, ideal after a cold afternoon building a snowman.

1 egg · 1 breakfast cup plain flour · 2 tsp sugar · 2 tsp baking powder · pinch salt · ¼ – ½ pint milk

✦

Beat egg in bowl, adding flour and milk alternately until you have a thick batter. Add sugar. Leave batter for half an hour before cooking. Before putting into an omelette pan, add two teaspoons of baking powder. Smear pan with buttered paper and heat. Pour on the mixture. When golden brown on one side, turn and cook the other side. Altogether about ten to fifteen minutes. Sprinkle icing sugar on top. Split and spread with butter, and eat while still hot.

Almond Paste

10 oz ground almonds · 5 oz castor sugar · 5 oz icing sugar ·
1 egg · 1 tblsp lemon juice · 1 tsp orange flower water · 1 tsp
rose water

❖

Place almonds, castor sugar and icing sugar in a bowl.
Beat up egg with liquids. Add to mixture and pound lightly.
Knead until smooth. Place almond paste on top of your cake,
and mould on to the sides, first dusting your hands with icing
sugar. Leave the cake in a tin for a few days before icing with
glacé or Royal icing.

❖

Meringue Mushrooms

To decorate the Christmas Log Cake

2 egg whites · 4 oz castor sugar

Beat the egg whites to peaks. Fold in the castor sugar. Make small mushroom tops with a teaspoon. Bake in a very cool oven for at least one hour. When ready, place on little stalks fashioned from rolls of boiled marzipan cut to suitable lengths.

Christmas Cake

8 oz sifted flour · 6 oz butter · 6 oz Barbados sugar · 1 lb sultanas ·
12 oz raisins · 4 oz glacé cherries halved · 2 oz almonds · 2 oz ground
almonds · 8 oz glace cherries · 4 oz candied peel shredded · 4 eggs ·
grated rind of 1 lemon · 1 tblsp black treacle · 1 tblsp golden syrup ·
1 tblsp brandy · 1 tblsp sherry · 1 tsp orange flower water · 1 tsp
rose water · 1 coffeespoonful ground cinnamon, ginger, nutmeg,
cloves · pinch of salt

❖

Sift the flour and salt. Put the butter and sugar into a clean
pan and stand in a warm place to soften. Put the fruit into
the flour. Add the peel, thinly shredded. Beat the butter &
sugar into a cream, adding the eggs one at a time, and beating
well after the addition of each egg. Add the flour and fruit
and mix well, moistening with the brandy, sherry, syrups
and flower water. Give it a final mix for several minutes.

Prepare a cake tin with a double thickness of greaseproof paper,
and spoon in the mixture. Set the oven at 350° Mark 4.
After one hour reduce the heat to 325° Mark 3, and cover
the top of the cake with a double thickness of greaseproof
paper. Time about two and a half hours. Test after two
hours by sticking a fine skewer in the centre. If it comes
out clean, the cake is done.

48

Never slam the oven door. Allow the cake to cool before turning out on to a wire rack.

When quite cold, wrap in greaseproof paper and store for one week. (Brush the cake all over with an apricot jam glaze and leave until set.

NOTE : for easy measurement, warm the treacle and syrup first.

Royal Icing

1 lb icing sugar · 2 egg whites · strained juice of half lemon

Sift the icing sugar. Whisk the egg whites until they are frothy, then gradually add the icing sugar, beating thoroughly. Continue beating until the mixture stands in peaks. Like glacé icing, this looks well when forked up into peaks resembling snow caps, after spreading on cake!

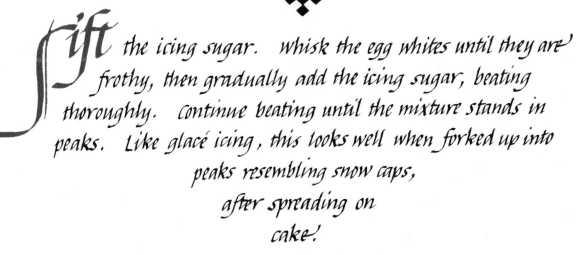

Christmas Biscuits

this is a good recipe for children to make for their grandparents, aunts & cousins

1 lb butter · 2 eggs · ½ lb sugar · 2 -3 tsp nutmeg · 1 tsp salt · 2 tsp vanilla essence · 2 dsstsp milk · 1½ lb plain flour, sifted

Mix all the ingredients together in a large bowl. Form into a ball, and place in refrigerator to get cold before rolling out thinly - no more than ¼ inch. With a knife carefully cut out the letters to spell CHRISTMAS, and use to decorate the tea table, or hang them on the tree. These biscuits can be iced - red, white and green coloured icing makes them look very attractive. A complete set spelling out HAPPY CHRISTMAS makes a very pretty Christmas gift if laid out in a suitable box.

Christmas Shortbreads

6 oz plain flour · 5 oz sieved icing sugar · 4 oz soft butter · pinch of salt · cinnamon or ginger powder · a little castor sugar · set of party-biscuit cutters

Mix flour and butter together thoroughly, then add the icing sugar and pinch of salt. Mix again. Roll out onto floured board very carefully. The mixture is apt to crack, but be patient and press it together. They are delicious biscuits and well worth the trouble.

With the party-biscuit cutters, usually shaped like stars, Christmas trees and hearts, cut out the shapes. If these are not available, use a pointed knife, but this is more difficult. Be sure to use a wide palette knife to lift the biscuits off the board and place gently into a flat baking tin. Cook in a medium to hot oven for 10-15 minutes. Check after 10 minutes.

When ready, lift carefully out and again with the palette knife place on a wire tray to cool and sprinkle with the castor sugar while still hot.

Custard Biscuits

6 oz self raising flour · 3 oz icing sugar · 2 oz custard powder · 6 oz butter

✦

Knead all ingredients into a dough. Roll into walnut sized pieces and press onto a greased baking tray with a fork. Bake at Gas Nº 2½ for thirty to forty minutes. They should not be allowed to brown at all. Leave to cool before carefully removing from the tray.

Sweetmeats and Candies

Sweetmeats and candies in tempting profusion play a
large part in a child's Christmas. You can buy
sweet cutters and tiny paper cases, and with the help
of greaseproof paper, tissue paper, tinfoil, sequins and
tinsel and coloured ribbons, along with attractive
cardboard boxes, these can make charming gifts.

Piled high in pyramids, or artfully arranged in suitable
dishes, sweets are splendidly eye-catching table centre
decorations, or use them on side tables or on wide
window sills.

Plain Fondant

This is a basic fondant recipe which can be used to make a variety of sweets by simply adding different colourings & flavourings

1 lb icing sugar · white of 1 egg · 1 dsstsp water · 1 tsp lemon juice · pinch cream of tartar

Rub sugar through fine sieve, put into bowl and add cream of tartar. Mix well. Stir in water and lemon juice. Whip egg white until stiff and work into sugar gradually until it is a thick paste and can be kneaded. If too dry, add more egg white. Turn onto board which has been dusted with icing sugar and knead for about five minutes, then leave to settle for about one hour.

Coconut Kisses add coconut and pink colouring.

Fruit Creams add chopped glacé cherries or other glacé fruits, and finely chopped blanched almonds. Can also be covered with melted chocolate.

Sugar Mice

2 lbs granulated sugar · ⅔ pint water · 1 dsstsp liquid glucose,
or, ½ tsp cream of tartar [prevents sugar from crystallising] ·
pieces of fine string for tails

Heat with water on a low heat. This process must not be hurried
when bringing to boil. Stir until sugar dissolves, add glucose or
cream of tartar, cover and bring to boil again. Heat to 235°–240°.
If no thermometer is available, drop a small amount into icy water.
If this forms a small ball which flattens when put on a plate, it is
ready. Pour immediately on to a dampened marble slab or hard
board. Leave to cool and stir with wooden spatula or spoon until
smooth. Divide and add colouring to each section if wished, or
leave white. Stir each section in turn [if they have been coloured]
until a lump has been formed. Mould into small roly-poly
shapes with a sharp end for the head. Insert a piece of string
for the tail, using a thin skewer, then smoothing the join. Pinch
out the ears, mark the mouth, and indicate the eyes with a grain
of chocolate.

Sugar mice can also be made from plain fondant. Instead of using
chocolate for the eyes, one could use the silvered sugar balls
for cake decoration.

Truffles

8 oz icing sugar · 3 oz butter · 2 oz ground almonds · 2 oz chocolate ·
almond essence · rum essence · icing sugar to dredge · white of 1
egg · chocolate vermicelli

Beat the butter, almond and rum essence. Stir in the
sieved icing sugar and ground almonds. Melt the chocolate
and when cool beat into the mixture. Roll into small balls,
leave to become firm, then coat with beaten egg white and roll
in chocolate vermicelli.

Marshmallows

10 oz sugar · ¼ pint water · 1 dsstsp glucose · ¾ oz gelatine ·
3 tblsp orange flower water made up to ¼ pint with water ·
white of one egg

❖

Boil the sugar, water and glucose to 260°F. Melt the
gelatine in water and orange flower water. When ready,
pour the boiled sugar into the pan with the gelatine and
mix well. Add stiffly beaten white of egg and whisk until
stiff. Beat with a wooden spoon and leave in pan until cold.
Re-heat for one minute and turn on to paper which has been
dusted with icing sugar. Dust all over with icing sugar and
leave for one hour. Cut into squares, using scissors, and
leave to dry.

Peppermint Creams

(Proceed as for sugar mice, and add a few drops of real peppermint essence, obtainable from chemist.

✦

Chocolate Liqueur Cherries

Glacé cherries · sherry liqueur or French brandy [the stronger the better] · chocolate chips · cocktail sticks

✦

Place whole cherries in bowl covered with chosen liquor. Cover with a plate and leave several days. Strain. This surplus liquor is ideal to use for the Christmas icecream. (Put cherries on cocktail sticks and sink into the chocolate mixture which has been thoroughly softened on top of a warm oven.

Coffee Creams

6 oz icing sugar · 1 oz ground almonds · 1 tblsp cream · a few drops of orange flower water or vanilla · white of one egg · coffee essence

Sieve icing sugar and ground almonds. Add cream and flavouring. Whisk egg white and add sufficient to the icing sugar and almonds to make a stiff paste. Work in enough coffee essence to make a light brown. Leave for a few hours. Roll out gently with a sugared rolling pin, and cut into shapes with a sweet cutter. Place on a board and leave to dry. Half a blanched almond or a piece of crystallised fruit can be pressed onto each sweet for decoration.

Turkish Delight

(These make a beautiful present

1 oz gelatine · 8 fluid oz water [barely] · 2 oz almonds · 1 oz chopped crystallised cherries · 1 lb sugar · icing sugar · flavouring · colouring

❖

In half a cup of the water, leave the gelatine to soak. Blanch the almonds and chop coarsely. Cut the cherries into small pieces. Dissolve the sugar in the remaining water and boil until it makes a soft ball when tested in cold water. Heat the gelatine and add it to the mixture. Add the nuts and cherries and any flavouring and colouring desired. Pour into oiled tins until about an inch thick. When cold, cut into cubes and roll in icing sugar.

Suggested flavouring: orange, lemon, raspberry etc.

Coffee Bonbons

1lb icing sugar · white of 1 egg · shelled walnuts or blanched almonds · 1 tsp castor sugar · pinch cream of tartar · coffee essence · 10 drops approx. vanilla essence

Sieve the icing sugar and mix in the cream of tartar. Beat egg white until stiff. Put half into a separate dish and add enough coffee essence to make it brown. Stir into the icing sugar and add vanilla. Add more white of egg until it is a stiff but pliable paste. Knead until mixture is smooth. Sugar your hands and form pieces of the paste into small balls. Press half a walnut or half a split almond on each side. Roll in castor sugar and leave to dry about twentyfour hours.

Candied Fruits

1lb canned or preserved fruit · 20 oz sugar · water · [suitable fruits –
apricots · plums · cherries · peaches · pineapples · greengages]

❖

Take the syrup from 1lb of canned or bottled fruit and make up
by adding water to ½ pint. Place in a saucepan with ½ lb of
sugar. Heat, stirring constantly until sugar is dissolved, then
bring to boil and remove from heat.

Put the fruit in a bowl and pour syrup over it, making sure it is
completely covered. Keep the fruit under by placing a saucer
on top, and allow to stand for 24 hours.

NOW strain off the syrup, add 2 oz of sugar, heat gently to dissolve
the sugar and bring to boiling point. Again pour over fruit and
leave for 24 hours.

Repeat this process two more times, adding 2 oz more sugar each
time. On the fifth day remove the syrup and add 3 oz of sugar,
heat till dissolved, then return the fruit and boil 3–4 minutes.
Now put the fruit and syrup back in the bowl and leave 48 hours.
Repeat this last process: the syrup should be like thick honey, & the
fruit should soak in it another 3–4 days. If the syrup is too thin,
add 3 oz sugar and re-boil. Finally, drain off syrup, drain fruit on
a wire tray, then place in a very cool oven for about 3 days until dry.
Pack in suitable boxes, using waxed paper. Keep dry & in dark.

62

Barley Sugar

1 lb loaf sugar · ½ pint water · ½ lemon · pinch cream of tartar.
a little oil or butter

Put the sugar and water into a strong saucepan, and stir over gentle heat until the sugar has dissolved. Add cream of tartar and bring to the boil. After five minutes remove from heat and add one dessertspoon of lemon juice. Boil to 300°F., that is, until it is brittle when a little is tested in cold water. Drop the mixture onto an oiled tin in very small quantities, or cut out thinly over tin. When cooled a little, cut it into short strips with well-oiled scissors, twist and leave till cold.

63

Crystallised Flowers

Flowers · 3 tsp gum arabic crystals [not powder] · 3 tblsp rose or orange water · castor sugar · vegetable colouring

In a small screw top jar place 3 teaspoons of gum arabic, cover with 3 tablespoons of rose or orange water, and leave two to three days to dissolve. Shake occasionally.

With a small camel hair brush, paint the solution on each flower, carefully covering each petal, calyx and part of the stem. Any part left bare will not keep. Take apart large loose flowers and do each petal separately; re·assemble when finished.

Dredge lightly several times with castor sugar until you are sure the flower is quite covered. Dry thoroughly on muslin or greaseproof paper in some warm place, like a linen cupboard, for about 24 hours. Large flat flowers can project over the edge of a shelf, anchored by the stems. Store in the dark in a cardboard box.

A very little vegetable colouring in the solution makes the flowers appear brighter, but don't overdo it. Suitable flowers are, roses, sweet peas, primroses, violets, cowslips, plum, apple and pear.

Edible Frosting
Make up the same gum solution, but do not add vegetable colouring. Paint this on to warm plates, and dry in a cool oven. Scraped off, this makes glittering "frost".

Sugar Plums

½ lb tenderised prunes · castor sugar

Cover the prunes with boiling water and allow to stand for five minutes. Drain, cover again with fresh boiling water, and leave for a further five minutes. Drain again. Weigh the prunes and place in a saucepan with an equal quantity of sugar. Barely cover with water and slowly bring to the boil. Simmer until the prunes are tender and the syrup thickens, stirring occasionally [five to ten minutes]. Lift prunes one at a time from the syrup and roll in castor sugar. LEAVE overnight to dry in a warm place, then store in a jar!

Marrons Glacé

2 lbs chestnuts · lemon juice · 1 tsp glucose · 1 pint water · 2 lbs sugar · vanilla essence · pinch cream of tartar

Score the chestnuts, put into boiling water and boil for five minutes. Skin, and place in warm water to which a squeeze of lemon juice has been added. Boil very gently until tender. Lift out carefully and dry well. Boil half a pint of water, one pound of sugar, and a teaspoon of glucose to 218°F. Add vanilla essence and pour this over the chestnuts, cover, and stand in a warm place for two days. On the third day drain the chestnuts well, and prepare a syrup consisting of the remaining one pound of sugar, half pint of water and pinch of cream of tartar. Boil these ingredients to 230°F. and when syrup is ready put in the chestnuts and just bring to the boil. Lift out chestnuts and drain well. Put on a rack to dry in a warm place. When quite dry, prepare the glacé syrup.

Glacé Syrup

Boil together to 225°F. one pound sugar, 1 teaspoon glucose and ¼ pint water. Add chestnuts and bring to the boil again. Stir the syrup till it grains slightly. Lift out the chestnuts and place on an oiled tin.

Boiled Marzipan Shapes

1 lb granulated sugar · 6 fluid oz water [approx.] · 3/4 lb ground almonds · 2 egg whites · juice of 1/2 lemon · 4 tblsps icing sugar · colouring ·

✤

Place the sugar and water in a saucepan and dissolve over gentle heat. Bring to the boil and cook steadily to 240°. Remove the pan from heat and beat till opaque. Stir in ground almonds and the lightly beaten egg whites. Cook for 2 - 3 minutes. Add colour and turn on to plastic board. Knead and roll flat. Cut out leaf shapes, berries, stars, moons and other decorative motifs.

Crystallised Fruit

a quick method

Tinned fruit - pineapple and apricot are ideal · fresh fruit cooked very gently; it must be firm and unbroken

Put the fruit on a wire cake rack and place in a large baking tin. Boil two lbs of granulated sugar to one pint of water and/or juice. Boil until 220°F, 104°C. Remove from heat and allow to cool. Pour the syrup over the fruit and set in a cool room. A thick sugary crust will form. Take out the fruit, drain, and place very gently on a wire rack to dry, turning occasionally until completely dry.

For presents, place them in rows in sweet cases in an attractive box.

A sugar thermometer should be used but is not essential.

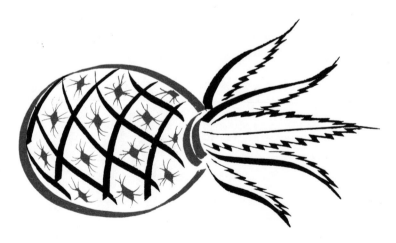

Sugared Mint Leaves

Lay the mint leaves on a Swiss roll tin, brush with unbeaten raw egg white, then sprinkle thickly with granulated sugar and dry out completely in the oven at 240°F. [Gas 1/4]. Store in an airtight tin until needed.

Cinnamon Toast

Mix butter and powdered cinnamon, spread on hot toast and eat immediately. (Delicious on a cold night with mulled wine.

Christmas Wine
Julglögg

This is a delicious traditional Christmas drink from NORWAY

1 bottle aquavit · 2 bottles burgundy · 3 oz stoned raisins · 1 tblsp cardamom seeds · 4 oz sugar · 6 whole cloves · 3" stick of cinnamon · 1 piece lemon rind

Pour the burgundy and half the aquavit into a saucepan. Stir in the raisins and sugar. Make a muslin bag for the spices and lemon rind, place in the saucepan and cover. Bring to the boil very slowly and barely simmer for half an hour. Add the remaining aquavit just before removing it from the heat. Remove the muslin bag, and at the last minute ignite with a match.

Pour into punch glasses and drink immediately –!

Egg Nog

It has been a traditional custom in North America for many years to drink Egg Nog on Christmas Day, although this ancient custom had its origins in Europe

1 bottle whisky [better with Irish whiskey] · 1lb white castor sugar · 2 doz eggs · grated rind of at least 2 lemons · 1 pt milk · 1pt cream · 2 nutmegs

The quantities given here are simply a guide. Some people will prefer less whisky and no cream, or less sugar and more cream etc.. Keep tasting as you mix it and keep a steady hand. Start off with six eggs and a few ounces of sugar, the grated rind of half a lemon, and small amounts of milk and cream. Whisk very thoroughly and start tasting. Add the rest of the ingredients as you see fit, and when you have given it a final long whisk in a beautiful bowl, finely grate a whole nutmeg over the top. Ladle it into wine or punch glasses, and before drinking, grate a touch of nutmeg over each Egg Nog to achieve an irresistible aroma.

Whisky Punch

6 oz lump sugar · 3 lemons · 1½ pints of boiling water · 1 pint of whisky

Rub four of the lumps of sugar on to the rind of the three lemons until all of the yellow rind is rubbed off on to the sugar. Put into a large bowl with the rest of the sugar. Squeeze the juice of two lemons over the sugar, and pour on the boiling water. Stir well until all the sugar is dissolved. Add one pint of whisky, heated but not boiled, and serve hot.

Mulled Wine

a warming drink for carol singers

1 litre red wine · ½ pint water · 1 orange stuck with cloves, cut in half · ½ lb sugar · 1 lemon, sliced · 1 cinnamon stick · powdered cinnamon to taste

PUT all the ingredients into a pan and heat, but do not boil. Keep at this temperature for thirty minutes, stirring occasionally to make sure the sugar has dissolved.

SERVE very hot, with a little cinnamon powder on top of each glass.

Wassail Cup
with Roast Chestnuts

The traditional hot drink passed from hand to hand in a loving cup just as the roast chestnuts are popping.

To make Wassail Cup:

"Boil three pints of ale; beat six eggs, the whites and yolks together; set both to the fire in a pewter pot; add roasted apples, sugar, beaten nutmegs, cloves and ginger; and, being well brewed, drink it while hot."

From the Royal Kitchen in 1633,
T. G. Crippen, "Christmas and Christmas More," 1923, p.101

Hunting Flask

for a cold Boxing Day!

Take equal quantities of whisky and Drambuie and a dash of Stone's Green Ginger. Put all the ingredients in a pan and heat, but do not boil. Pour immediately into a flask.

Cherry Liqueur

1 lb Morello cherries · 1 lb black cherries · ½ lb preserving sugar · 1 small stick of cinnamon · 12 cloves · 1 bottle of brandy

❖

Remove the stalks from the cherries, crush the stones and the cherries, and put them into a large bottle with the sugar, cloves and cinnamon. Over this pour the brandy. Cork the bottle lightly and leave for at least two weeks. After this interval, strain the liquid and pour into small bottles. Cork securely and store until Christmas. (Don't forget to stick on each bottle a beautiful label decorated with cherries and leaves.

This can be made with Morello cherries only, but then it becomes more like cherry brandy. (For this, you should halve the amount of sugar. They both make excellent Christmas presents.

Christmas Tradition
Christmas Pudding

Everyone in the family should stir the Christmas Pudding, and while they are doing so, make a wish. A ring, a thimble and a silver coin should be stirred in at the end. The ring means a wedding, the thimble a life of single blessedness, and the coin brings fortune to the finder.

At Christmas lunch, a sprig of the best holly with the brightest berries is stuck on the top of the pudding, then brandy is heated in a spoon above a candle and when ignited poured over the pudding just as you carry it into the dining room.

The Kissing Bough

This ancient decoration was the traditional centrepiece of the Christmas festivities until Prince Albert brought in the Christmas Tree just over a hundred years ago. But it is one of the most glorious decorations imaginable, and its purpose is to hold the bunch of mistletoe whose purpose gives this Bough its name.

The Bough can be made in a globe or sphere shape, or for a low cottage ceiling it may be in the shape of a crown.

Make the frame out of a strong but pliable wire. It should last for many years. For the globe, make five circles of wire. [see drawing.] Use only one type of evergreen to cover the framework - ideally rosemary or box, since they grow tightly. Bind the branches onto the wire with a strong but fine thread. Take seven shining red apples and fasten them by the stalk to a long length of red or blue silken ribbon. Place the apples in the centre of the globe; for the crown, hang six apples round the edges and one in the centre. Bind the bottom eight candles with fine wire, placing them in between the eight pieces of wire crossing the "equator". Use long white candles of slow burning wax [they have suitable ones in church shops]. Wind ribbons in contrasting colours up the candles in a spiral, placing little pins in appropriate places so that the ribbon can be snipped off as the candle burns down.

78

Lastly, tie a bunch of mistletoe at the bottom of the globe!
  (For the crown, tie it with a long ribbon from the top, making
  sure that some of it falls below the centre [see drawing].
  Many delicate objects can be added to the frame: tiny gifts
  tied with tinsel, little mirrors, tangerines, bows and little birds.

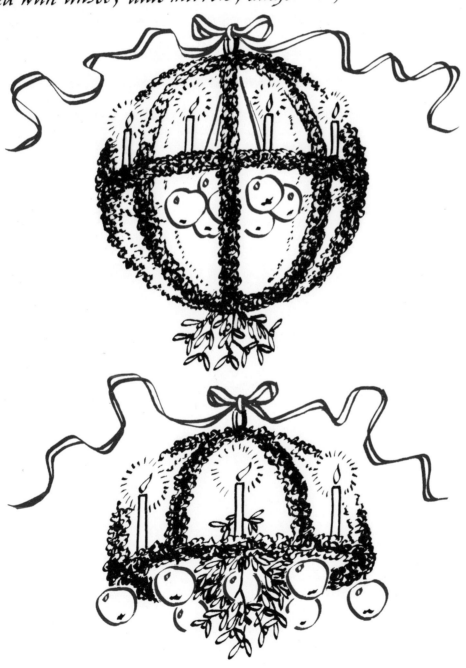

A Holly Garland

An exquisite way to decorate a formal room ✳

A berry and a leaf of holly are strung alternately on a thread, the needle piercing the leaf at each end to keep it flat. Long chains are then hung round the walls in shallow loops, with short vertical pieces hanging between. To be really effective, the whole room should be treated in this manner.

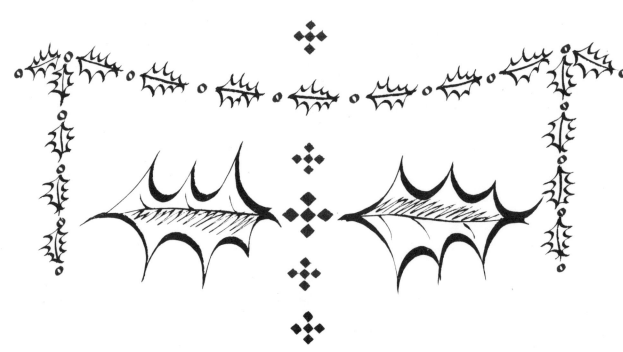

✳ *Invented by Rex Whistler*
from "The English Festivals", by Laurence Whistler

Snapdragon

FOR an exciting treat after dinner on Christmas night, place into a flat dish a heap of raisins and roasted almonds. Cover them with brandy, turn off all the lights, and ignite. From the flaming plate everyone snatches the almonds and raisins, and when they are all gone, throw salt over the excess brandy, and it will expire in a green flash of light.

Decoration

Every available area in the dining room should be piled high with pyramids of tangerines, apples, frosted grapes, marrons glacé; with dainty dishes of crystallised fruits, mint leaves and miniature marzipan models. Surround the dishes with garlands of holly or evergreens. Place home-made sweets wrapped in shiny paper tied with coloured ribbons in between the greenery.

Yuletide Wreath

This traditional decoration is hung on your front door. Use the same method of construction as for the Kissing Bough - wire covered with holly, yew, fir or any available evergreens. Suspend a colourful centrepiece, here Christmas tree baubles; but use any suitable objects, fruit etc., and finish with strands of tinsel.

Metric Conversion

1 ounce	equals	28 grams	1 teaspoon	equals	2·5 ml
2 ounces	"	56 grams	1 tablespoon	"	15 ml
3 ounces	"	85 grams	1 dessertspoon	"	25 ml
4 ounces	"	113 grams	1 pint	"	500 ml
8 ounces	"	227 grams	3/4 pint	"	375 ml
16 ounces	"	454 grams	1/4 pint	"	125 ml

These are near approximations, since fractions of a gram are omitted for the sake of clarity

Index

Salads · Vegetables

Puddings · Desserts

Drinks